AF390724

What lies behind the smile of
a single-eyed heart?

It hides a small, intimate, four-room house with diffused light and

the scent of love.

It hides a house with one eye.

Through the eye of the house can be seen

half the sun,

half the moon,

half an apple

and half a pear.

The other halves haunt the world.

Their hearts seek them out,

just as

my one-eyed heart seeks its half.

BETWEEN

love

&

unlove

Louisa Rehbein

Looking through my old things, I discovered a photograph

yellow, bent, old.

In it, the faces of my grandparents.

Two old chairs held two mountains of strength and gentleness;

Two rough, hard-working hands reaching for each other,

photographing themselves together.

The picture tells of their love.

There, in the yellow, bent, old picture lies my ancestral love.

From there it comes and I carry it on,

with you by the hand, my love.

Knock on the door of a wall's heart

and you'll realise that its heart doesn't answer...

Touch the heart of a wall

and you'll feel it's cold...

Bring your ear close to the heart of the wall

and you'll find it doesn't beat...

Ask the wall about its love!

It'll tell you it's made of stone...

You turned your back on Love

and it came out in front of you.

You turned again,

but love found you back.

You tried to hide from love

behind a closed door,

but love burst through it

to tell you it won't give you peace.

You try to hide and you can't.

How strong do you have to be to accept love?

How strong do you have to be to be honest with love?

How strong do you have to be to cherish your love?

Godly strong.

Ask the sea what love is...

The waves will answer...

Love is that frantic movement

free and disorderly

that metamorphoses your being

with the power of cold, foamy water

that caresses, striking in haste,

the solitary rock in the middle

of the blue vastness.

If love were chocolate,

people would melt

in a whole flood of sweetness and flavor.

They say love is felt with the heart.

but I feel love with my arms,

I feel it with my lips.

I feel it with my skin.

All my senses

feel ecstatic

in the tumult of love.

My heart ONLY flutters with joy

feeling my happy being.

What is the soul?

Mine is a flower,

whose petals love to be pampered by the warm sun,

love to feel the restless hum of the bees,

love to touch the bright green grass,

carried by the breeze of a friendly wind.

My soul is a flower that loves to sway,

moved by the soft touch of some gentle words,

that loves to be caressed by the gentle feel of another flower.

My soul is a flower that loves peace.

Love strives for victory despite the constant pursuit of unlove ...

... and as long as life shall be,

there will be love.

There'll be sick love,

there'll be tormented love,

there'll be dirty love,

there'll be toxic love,

there'll be Black love,

Red,

Green,

Blue,

or Yellow.

There'll be the love of pure souls

and of bleeding souls;

There'll be the love of white minds

and dark ones;

There'll be love that is kind and warm;

There'll be love that is vengeful and cold.

In love lie deep feelings

that, controlled by a troubled mind,

give birth to UNLOVE.

What's hidden in the love of a teaspoon of
honey that tenderly sweetens the love of tea
born from the mingling of flower souls, that in a
warm embrace, have given it all their colors?

How does love Blossom between a flower and a thorn?!

She tells him he's scary.

He tells her she's fragile.

She tells him he's dangerous.

He tells her she's fearful.

She tells him he's unfriendly.

He tells her she's demanding.

She tells him he's tough.

He tells her she doesn't know him.

She tells him he doesn't bloom.

He tells her he's strong.

She tells him that he has no color.

He tells her he's got color in everything around him.

She tells him what's around him is not his.

He tells her that he can grasp the surroundings.

She tells him that she doesn't like to be grasped.

He tells her that even LOVE is grasping.

She tells him that LOVE cannot be grasped.

He turns around and walks away,

leaving her to understand THE GRASP...

The Lost Path of Love

In love are embraced the sky,

the sun,

the moon,

and the stars.

In love are embraced the sea,

the earth,

the grass,

the flowers,

the trees,

and the air.

In love are embraced the love,

the hard feelings,

and the sorrows.

In love is ALSO embraced the HATE.

Hate is Love.

But it's a Love that's sick.

A Love that has lost its mind.

A love that must be helped to find its way.

It's a Love written BACKWARDS, that has lost the meaning of its

next life and is left incomplete.

Dear sick LOVE,

EVOL-VE!

In its rage to find its mate,

my love has run away,

but stumbled and fell.

My love is hurt.

It came back to me disappointed and scratched.

It says it doesn't look the same and loneliness transfigures it.

Now she's bandaged and carefully nursed

by a kind mother's warm soul.

How can I teach my love to stop running?!

Dear Love, when you want to tell me something,
pat me gently on the heart.
I'll bend down and listen to you.
Then, whisper to me the words that could provide you peace.
I'll guide you with slow, steady steps,
to make sure that you'll be safe.

My love escapes

My love escapes through my arms.

It wants to hold you and hug you tight,

in its intense feeling.

My love escapes through my lips.

They want to touch you and burn you with their intense desire.

My love escapes through my skin.

My skin captures energies and transforms them into intense

feelings,

giving my body

the sensation of absolute love.

My body needs your love.

It's me.

It's me and my love.

My love is soft.

Soft and fierce.

My love is sweet

Sweet and bitter.

My love is calm.

Calm and restless.

My love is precious.

Precious and free.

My love is warm.

Warm and temperate.

My love is desire.

Desire and refusal.

My love is up.

Up and down together.

My love is mysterious

Mysterious and revealed.

My love is waiting.

Waiting and impatience.

My love is peace.

Peace and war.

My love is plus.

Plus and minus, together.

My love is YOU.

You and ME.

I close my eyes and think of you.

I see your reflection in the old farmhouse window.

Your eyes gleam as you look at me. I move closer.

I feel your heart.

It feels as if it wants to burst from your chest,

as if it longs for a grand rendezvous.

Your arms, around me.

You radiate warmth, and I feel your heat engulfing me.

I step back and let you succumb to your primal instincts.

I can't identify love in your tender desire.

I'm leaving...

"I'll see you again," you say.

I look at you and smile,

knowing SHE desires you.

And you, you desire ME.

It's a threesome I'm excluding myself from.

I know what you want,

but there's a battle raging within you.

Something's stirring in your heart.

She's there, I'm not.

She's near, I'm not.

She's pursuing you, I'm not.

She desires you, I don't.

She follows her interests, I don't.

She doesn't love you, I do.

Farewell, my LOVE!

Heartful curse

If I were to gaze into your eyes,

I'd willingly surrender to their depth,

And I'd hope to remain there,

So that your gaze would forever hold me,

In the forefront of your thoughts.

You're asking for a kiss.

I strangely still can feel you...

I sit in your arms and feel your frustration.

You want me.

But that's all.

I feel like you've prepared a plan B.

I leave, she stays.

She'll always be there for you.

A little for you and mostly for her.

You're naive.

I'm not.

You'll get what you want.

But not from me.

We remain friends, just as you don't like it...

I left...

I left you alone.

Alone among those many people.

Without her, but with her in your mind.

She was your backup plan, I knew that.

Still,

I liked the way you held my head in your hands.

and kissed me on the forehead every time you saw me again.

I liked the comfort I felt around you.

I'd probably feel the same today.

I loved your arms full of emotion.

I loved your innocent heart.

I loved your touch and your awkwardness.

Beyond any hidden intention, your flesh revealed your secrets.

It gave you away.

Your body didn't seem to help you.

It didn't know how to lie.

You were trying to control yourself.

And you suddenly became malicious.

You understood I wouldn't give in.

I was going to leave.

Your heart was screaming for me.

It struggled to know me...

My heart is still sorry...

You used to call...

You used to call and listen to my voice, silent as a whisper,

No words spoken, your breath a mystery.

On the other end, a tranquil silence prevailed,

Was that enough to quench your thirst?

I try to envision how it felt for you,

Recall that message on New Year's Eve,

"I offer you 365 angels, guardians of your days,"

Do you remember?

Unsigned, a hidden number ...

You struggled to move beyond the past,

Our temperaments clashed, my exuberance against your

introversion,

My levity and capriciousness met your solemnity,

Perhaps you judged without truly knowing, driven by hearsay .

But judgment won't mend a heart smitten with LOVE,

Is she still a there with her burdens,

or have your troubles merged into one?

I took my love in my hands,

nestling it close,

nosing its tender warmth.

I was glad to have saved it,

for my love knows no pain.

Love must be painless,

for where there's suffering, love wanes.

And my love shines bright,

for love can be nothing else.

I vibrate with love.

Love has a life of its own.

It doesn't care about your frail body,

your distant gaze,

or the book left unread on your nightstand.

Love has its own eyes,

its own body,

and its own purpose.

Love seems like another being hidden within you.

Love doesn't listen, doesn't speak, doesn't judge.

Love doesn't offend, doesn't argue, doesn't gaze into the mirror.

Love doesn't seek elegance, luxury, or opulence.

Love doesn't need grand houses, expensive cars,

or precious clothing.

Love walks naked,

revealing itself naturally,

free from constraints, complexes, or frustrations.

Love is the purest feeling of all

because love cannot be feigned.

I'm standing on the bank of a mountain river.

In the middle, I see a heart-shaped stone.

The water seems to pass by indifferently.

But I see how in the carved heart

are gathered all the unspoken mysteries of the trees

all the hidden longings of autumn leaves

all the brightness of the sun that cuts with its gleam

the quiet course of the river.

There, in that heart of stone

I locked my feelings,

so I could listen to yours

in the whispers of that young water's murmur.

Love has its own identity.

Its own religion.

Its own language.

Its own wisdom.

Its own science.

Its own conscience.

Love has its own superiority.

I keep my eyes open and I see you.

I see you behind my open eyes.

I can still feel you.

Sometimes I think of you, but not in the same way.

It's been so long, that something in me has forgotten you.

I have no emotion.

I have no desire.

You're just there, in my passing thoughts.

When a love has no place next to your love,

step aside and make room for it to pass.

Maybe that love is looking for someone else.

They seem to devour themselves unhindered under the old gaze of

the falcon chestnut...

Just the two of them.

On a bench.

In the park.

Their carnal need to merge

is strong,

while Love feels crushed by the savagery of their lustful bites.

I continue my search...

I know a lost love is looking for me.

Or I, a lost being, am looking for IT.

It's not our time yet.

I clench my fist and imagine that I have contained within it a silent
love.
I close my eyes and imagine that I have enclosed within them a love
that runs playfully away from its mate.
I bring my lips together and imagine that in the warmth of my hot
mouth now lies a love that used to dance frantically before me.
What would I do with all the loves of the universe, if I could contain
them all within me?
What would all the loves of the universe do together?
I don't know.
I don't even know if there are more loves
or if there's only one Love dissipated to infinity.
I open my fist and release Love.
I open my eyes and let Love run.
I open my lips and let Love continue her dance.
Love is not a prisoner.

I dreamt of love.

It was a big heart drawn by a child

on a white sheet of paper.

It was red, and there, on the paper, the red love that gave life to the

Heart, was cheekily outlining it.

Instinctively,

Children know that love has no boundaries.

Two frail, dry hands, like crumpled papers in disarray,
Gently clasp each other
And tread the path of memories.

Two faint shadows, traced upon the youthful grass,
Contemplate the bustling life within a nest.

Two muted voices, burdened by the passage of time,
Shyly rediscover their maternal grace.

I sense a serenity frozen in time,
A tender, pure, and gentle feeling;
I perceive a beauty never seen before,
I sense Love.

That Love, revered by two golden souls,
of two paper bodies...

I recently met

a wounded Love.

I didn't know what to say,

for there are no words to comfort

a wounded Love.

How unhappy can who does not know Love be?

How unhappy can who does not accept Love be?

How unhappy can who does not want Love be?

How unhappy can who ignores Love be?

How unhappy can who mocks Love be?

How unhappy can who thinks they can stop Love be?

How unhappy can who thinks they can defeat Love be?

How unhappy can who thinks Love can be his alone be?

How unhappy can who laughs at Love be?

How unhappy can who leads Love into nothingness be?

So unhappy!

Thousands of figures walk up and down the streets.

I look behind them trying to understand their meaning.

I see a frozen face, dripping, a steaming tear.

There's love and unlove all in one.

There is suffering, a sign of unloving.

Nor does the tear that furrows the chilled cheek seem to be of

happiness.

How does a frozen love warm itself?

How does the Love know how to watch out itself from the Unlove?

It doesn't.

But Love and Unlove are two independent feelings.

There is no communion between them.

Nor do they recognize each other.

Love doesn't like Unlove

and

Unlove does not like Love.

But what is Unlove?

Unlove is everything Love is not.

You hid from me in silence.

You hid from me in the invisible.

You hid from me behind Her.

Not to see you.

Not to hear you.

The naivety of a man...

A woman's cunning.

Two glasses of wine and an empty bottle...

You move backward, letting your heart watch me...

At the same time, I move forward, letting your heart watch me,

whispering "You lost"...

At the core of my being is Love.

From there its rays shine upon me.

When I try to understand it, I borrow a ray

and write with it.

From time to time I write on a soul.

The one my Love chooses for me.

And though it seems infinite,

my love is all there,

where it chooses to live its story.

Don't judge your love!

Don't scold yourself for your love's choices!

Live them!

They are the experiences of your love and should be treasured.

Because of love, you can discover the Unlove, and thus

when your love finds fulfillment

by merging with another love,

you will know how to cherish your happiness.

On a pillow, a rose petal tells its story.

It is the story of the flower torn apart by unlove.

A story of sacrifice for Love ending in Unlove.

How does a rose petal know to cry?

A girl...

is walking lost...

toward the forest that open up before her and

seem to absorb her with its mystery,

for in the mysteries of the forest are hidden the mysteries of the

earth.

And in the mysteries of the earth are hidden the mysteries of the

world.

And in the mysteries of the world, the supreme mystery of the soul,

in its conventional form, the heart,

LOVE.

What she had lost, she was about to retrieve

for in the supreme mystery of the soul lie the mysteries of the

world,

and in the mysteries of the world lie the mysteries of the earth,

and the mysteries of the earth are hidden in the mysteries of the

forest,

that was about to set her free

on the path where the light was seen.

For here SHE finds her way.

Without the sun the earth would not feel its essence

Without the sun the sea would not feel its depth

Without the sun, the flower would not feel its fragrance

Without the sun, the sky would not find its brightness

Without the sun the fruit would remain unripe

Without the sun the moon would remain dark

Without the sun the day would remain night

Without the sun the world would not radiate happiness.

The sun is Love for everything that breathes our planet.

I love that little hand that used to hold tight

a teddy bear's ear,

hanging carelessly

and peeking out of the pink tulle dress,

that gracingly was adorning a blond little girl's body.

Suddenly, a need for closeness

called the other little hand to help.

The teddy bear,

held by two small hands,

now finds its love in a tight embrace.

Just until a mother's protective hand

grasps the little girl's right hand,

and the teddy bear, left in a single warm embrace,

remains listening with a lean ear

to the whisper of a tender heart,

where a young life was murmuring

LOVE.

Don't run to catch love, if it runs from you.

Don't bend down to pick up love if a love seems lost.

Don't strain to dream of love, if your dreams are tired.

Don't recite love, if the words are not yours.

Don't imagine love, if you'll keep it only in your imagination.

Don't draw love if you have no colors.

Don't strive to feel love when LOVE has its light dimmed.

Love is when it's looking for you,

Love is when it finds you,

Love is when you're awake,

Love is when you know the words to express it,

Love is when you feel it,

Love is a lot of color

and a lot of light.

Why do some people prefer Unlove?

Because Unlove is simple,

rudimentary, and indifferent.

Unlove has no obligations.

Unlove is safe.

Unlove gives no emotions.

Unlove does not feel.

Unlove is not desired.

Unlove is not crazy or tender.

It has no colors or flavors.

Unlove is the perfect attribute of a disguised unhappiness.

I sell my UNLOVE

because it degrades me,

it depersonalizes me,

it empties me.

Because it doesn't give me meaning,

because it leaves me with no feeling,

and keeps me still.

I sell my ugly Unlove

and I don't offer it.

I sell it

to the cowards,

to the wicked,

to the indifferent,

because they're rich...

...of EMPTINESS!

I don't know you

and you don't know me.

Our loves are looking for each other

and seem to want to know each other.

What about us?!

Our bodies are beyond love.

Our bodies host it but don't own it.

The love in us is independent and free.

The love in us makes its own decisions.

Our bodies are the perfect marionettes of our Love.

I see my Unlove looking long into the void...

It's trying to find that Something

to banish its loneliness.

But

Unlove doesn't know that what it seeks is unattainable.

Love hides from Unlove!

Why is suffering clear, when love is faded?

You paid me with soft, warm lips

on cold winter days

and in summer you left me

frozen...

In my immutable lips,

your kiss lay frozen,

in danger of melting under the hot summer sun.

I'm afraid it'll leak

and leave my lips colorless...

Now

my lips seek to soak up the roses.

SHE

A butterfly tickles a sad flower.

It tries to open its petals.

But the flower wanted to live in the need of suffering.

The flower wanted to live its suffering, to feel it, to release it

as it opened to a new day...

The flower had seen how an evil hand had fallen on the voice of its

happiness...

A cruel hand broke its love...

And left it alone...

Until a new love would join its petals to Tenderness.

Together, we reside in the ninth heaven,

merged in a love that both tears us apart...

A crimson aura surrounds us.

We move, and around us,

scents of love's perfume fill the air.

Roses bloom, releasing their magical scents.

We calm the sky, and the clouds take their sorrows away.

We soften the wind, which, in its fury, swirls around us,

leaving us beautiful and serene.

We temper the burning sun's fury,

finding shade in each other's embrace.

We merge with the flowers,

in communion with the universe;

We wish the cosmos to bear witness to our love.

I adorned her hair with a frangipani flower.

It's white and fragile.

It's so beautiful and pure.

It takes my words and cradles them in a warm voice,

as if they were coloring in it

all the iridescence of love...

The flower smiles at me.

It tells me she loves me...

I write my Unlove in a notebook with dark paper,

and I think there my Unlove will melt away

and stay in the old sheets.

Unlove is sensitive to light,

so I bind the notebook with a string,

for I have promised my Unlove intimacy.

I don't want my Unlove to upset me

I don't want it near me.

I don't want my Unlove to fool me.

Stay in the sheets, my Unlove,

And let me love!

I choose to climb the highest mountain

to release my suffering.

From there, it will either rise to the skies,

and dissipate,

or, maybe, it will let go down,

destructively.

I feign carelessness and improvise.

I breathe a sigh of relief in this unknown choreography.

The dance of my feelings is chaotic

They strike me and they drift away...

I refuse to take them back.

Leave me alone!

I don't want to hear war cries!

They're demeaning!

Theatrically, this show is a mad scramble

A reckless disarmament

A battle without a winner.

Fights are for fools.

They're a dishonorable fall from dignity.

When the Unlove growls, you turn your back and walk away.

Don't give it satisfaction.

Don't humiliate yourself.

When Love turns into Unlove,

accept it.

For otherwise it's like trying to color the sun...

Help me to understand Love.

Love,

unscramble my confusion!

Why are you, love, silent?

Why are you, love, not desperate?

Why do you, love, end?

Why are you, love, finite and infinite at the same time?

Why do you, love, yield to desire?

Why do you, love, not strike?

Why are you, love, shy and vulnerable?

Why do you, love, seek your ally in Boldness?

Why don't you, love, find your place once?

Why don't you, love, rely on me?

Love, do you love me?

How much love is in cheating?

On whose side is love in cheating?

Do you cheat out of love?

Do you cheat out of desire?

Do you cheat out of instinct?

A plate of fries and a chicken leg.

An apple and a glass of water.

Thank you, Love, but I'm tired.

Offer me a thick blanket to keep warm,

instead of answers!

You wanted me and chose to cheat me.

It's the tradition of dirty, unutterable soul harassment.

The whiteness of my beads unbalances you.

The black of my shoes throws you into despair.

You're cold and you seem to want me.

Your thought is of her, but you feel hungry for me.

While I'm here.

You didn't know how to win me.

Your words don't follow rules.

And they betrayed you.

You and I will never be HOME.

A leaf is the prisoner of a dry twig.

It stays still until the first gust of wind.

Then a cold, rushing rain drenches it.

Who's there for a prisoner leaf?

I give you my hand to take me away.

The steps hold me back.

They hold back my body.

Away, for them, is beside me.

My footsteps won't let me go any further.

I look at you and feel your disappointment.

I have wounded your pride.

I have.

Who am I?

The very same.

Who are you?

A different someone.

A very different someone ...other than who you want me to see.

You gazed at me with longing in your eyes,

yet your thoughts remained concealed, unspoken.

Words seemed your enemy.

Your tender eyes stroked the depths of my soul,

but they stood alone,

failing to beguile me.

I'm smart.

And beyond desire,

it will be always me.

It is important to understand that unloving hurts,

and,

by loving unloving,

we UNLOVE OURSELVES.

Dream and pursue those dreams,

In love, all things become attainable.

Give it a shot!

Be bold!

Strive!

But when you witness your adversary retreating,

move in the opposite direction,

for in a solo battle,

Defeat awaits.

Which one is the face of the sun?

Will it be the one facing me

or the one facing you?

To the Sun you don't speak,

The sun you don't sing to,

The Sun you don't write to.

The Sun doesn't get messages, because it burns them.

How can I reach the sun to tell it how much I love you,

and carry my love for you in a beam?

How to reach the sun and recite my love,

when the sun is busy making light?

How to sing to the sun the melody of my love,

when the sun shines his love?

In the sun all my love is contained.

Yellow,

Shining bright,

Warm,

Radiant,

All-embracing.

I give you my Sun, Love,

but take care not to burn yourself!

Give help to true love, mad and infuriated...

Give help to love that's misguided, weak, and lonely.

Give help to heavy love, and speak to it kindly.

Build a city for love.

Draw a house for love,

Without walls, without roofs,

Where many children run.

Purify your unloved love,

and give love new clothes.

Let love go out into the world

and enjoy life

with its passion!

I found written on a tear, Unlove.

U - NDER

N - OBLE

L - OVE

O - BEY

V - OW

E - MBRACE

I am rushing down a path,

because I've spotted my lonely love by a lake.

I walk hopelessly, aiming to surprise Love and bring about a joyful

touch.

But the lonely love cries whether from sorrow or elation.

It writes a long or short letter, you don't know,

to another love, be it new or old,

about a 'you and me.'

I can clearly see its accessories.

This love is painted in both vivid and muted hues,

Blessed by sunlight reflecting off the moon,

And cleansed by the serene waters of the silent lake.

However, that love remains silent.

I continue my walking.

No glance on me.

That love was not meant for me.

Two chubby children playing on the seashore.

They seem to be enjoying the mother's peace.

They are not looking for spiritual cures,

nor answers to hard questions.

They kick the waves crashing on the shore

with their tiny, unsteady feet.

Sometimes a more unfriendly wave

wash over them.

And they have fun.

They pick up the salty splashes in their hair and hugg each other

with every fall.

It is the need for support, for fellowship in play, for safety.

It is the need to be together and live in the moment.

That's what Love is about.

I have learned that the Unlove is not wanted.

After Unlove you should not run.

You don't want Unlove.

Unlove is an accident.

A broken used car.

A smelly apple

A crushed tomato.

I've learned that Unlove is anxious.

and that it has no cure.

Unlove,

you are the love-sick wretch

who hasn't found their cure ...

I found a symbol I've never seen before.

It was red, sharp, bright, and hot.

It was a hidden symbol on a string of beads,

a mark from a rainbow story.

It was a symbol unheard of, yet fascinating.

It was a symbol that annihilated my gaze.

It melted my heart

and softened my limbs.

It was a symbol that was complicated to live with

and yet complicated to let go of.

It was... You!

Allow your body to feel,

Let it truly understand.

Embrace both joy and pain,

both light and darkness,

both silence and thunder.

Give your body time to know you,

to comfort you,

when Love and Unlove clash.

Let your body relax into an embrace,

release itself in moments of resistance,

and accept its perfect imperfections.

Make your body your closest friend,

by calming its powerful anxieties,

and instilling life into it.

A delicate, fragile dark-haired woman spins frantically in her red
dress,
twirling in a perfect circle, embodying the wings of desire.
Across the street, two unmoving eyes,
accompanied by a tight smile and graying hair,
exude the scent of musk.

There's so much beauty in her angelic face.
There's so much desire in his unblinking gaze...

It's like water extinguishing the fire, light illuminating the darkness,
and the sun melting the ice.
I let the red dress write in the ether the love of hidden desire that
watched her insatiable.
A tale of desires converging, feeling by feeling, into a magical
autumn painting.

My hand's love story

My left hand commands my right hand to write.

My left hand wants my right hand to write a poem.

But my right hand doesn't want to.

It's too tired.

My left hand takes my right hand and lets it feel the paper.

My right hand slowly withdraws to my body.

It's shy and wants to keep its story to itself.

My left hand looks at it with no understanding.

If it could, my left hand would write its story,

but

what's the point of writing a lifeless, left-handed poem?

When you don't feel your own Love, don't try to feel someone else's.

I'm afraid to tell my heart to stop.

It's like cutting off its breath...

My heart is wild and adventurous

My heart likes you and me together.

My heart doesn't care about others

when it's living its moment.

My heart lives for itself and me

and together, sometimes, we are in search of a Heart...

I met a couple

She is asking him not to see the other woman.

Inside her there are turmoil, hard words, screaming, distrust,

disenchantment, worry, unhappiness...

He tells her that there's nothing between him and the other woman.

But she doesn't understand the past. The doubt and mistrust seem

to tear her apart.

Her weaknesses, bathed in the passion of love, make her angry and

her words boil over.

"Don't see her again, you understand, don't see her again!"

What are words worth to feelings?

How can you command his heart to want what your heart wants?

It's like drinking water, when the thirst is His, not yours.

Do you understand?

Love is not an Obligation.

Love is not an Order.

Love is not a Compulsion.

Love is diaphanous and tender.

Love, itself, is strong, courageous, and confident.

What you have, girl, is not Love.

It's Unlove! For you!

If my lips were to fall apart in love,

they would absorb your whole flesh and turn it into nothing more.

If my arms were to fall apart in love,

they would flood my whole body and bring you inside me.

If my eyes were to fall apart in love,

they would immortalize you in an unspoken thought.

If my smile were to fall apart in love,

it would know how to appear on magazine covers.

When my feeling floods you, rise and recompose yourself into

YOU!

That's what I need!

Give your old thoughts a rest.

Don't wake them up.

Thoughts like to be numbed.

Thoughts don't like to meddle, for they forget, they get lost.

Thoughts lose their identity, when you choose to awake them.

Let your thoughts live in the moment.

Each in its own time.

That's how you give your heart peace to feel,

your mind peace to understand,

your body strength to live.

I don't know if Love would ever tell me that you're Ugly.

That you're tall with crooked legs, thin lips, and close-set eyes.

My mind would tell.

My love sees you differently.

Do you wonder what my love sees beyond that truth?

Well, it sees an immense warmth squeezed into a smile penciled on

a soft face, coordinated with two arms that are painfully delicate

and soothing.

It sees how you hide your feelings and withdraw into yourself.

It sees how you're afraid to open up.

My love doesn't even wear glasses,

but,

it's like a tender ghost penetrating people, hearts, places...

And it's always good.

Still,

I'd love to know how my bespectacled love would see you.

There are three peonies in a vase on a table.

Two pink and one white.

Big, rich, fragrant.

I look at them and realize that the white one doesn't belong among

my pink peonies.

No matter how I place them, it doesn't get in the middle.

How can the white peony get in the middle?

It feels this need, but it doesn't know that the two pink peonies can

suffocate it with their beauty, with their gentleness, with their many

curled petals.

Is my white peony in danger?

It's not so beautiful, perhaps not so tender, and it doesn't have so

many curled petals.

My white peony is almost bald. It's tall and smeared with pollen

dots on the stamens that break up its mediocrity.

My pink peonies look at it shyly, but they know that ONE never

divides into TWO.

Don't try to share a love, it won't be yours or the one you're thinking

of sharing it with.

It will end up finding another host, all its own.

When he loves her, his love is hers.

When she loves him, her love is his.

What could He and She do with love?

It's simple. They could give it two hearts.

That's where love is known to feel best.

Then they could give it two bodies.

That's where love is known to make its home.

Then they could give it a face.

There it is known that love finds expression.

Then they could give it sap.

There it is known that love begets love...

I once encountered an Unlove.

It was a pure, transformed Love. By choice.

It had once been love.

That love had the misfortune of not understanding.

That love had chosen wrongly, at some point, another love that made it suffer.

And in its suffering, the Unlove of now, the Love of then, took revenge in death.

The Love that became Unlove killed.

It killed something it had no power to choose.

It killed the buds of the union of two loves, which could be its children.

Unlove, you were cursed so to remain...

If love is felt in the heart,

Where is Unlove felt?

What does love care about jewels and expensive clothes?!

What does love care about big houses and fancy cars?

What does love care about exotic vacations and bank accounts?

Do you think you can buy Love?

Do you know you're actually buying Unlove?

Your pride or, perhaps, your unbridled love has a salutary desire.

But do you think that as you feel, another may not feel and no material thing can induce that feeling?

Be rich in heart and take pride in that, not in the wealth of the world.

In wealth, there is no Love.

In wealth, there can be work and giving. But when there is work and giving there is intelligence.

And if there is intelligence, there is understanding.

Whoever is rich through work, dedication, and intelligence understands that not everything in life is for sale.

Love isn't!

Health isn't!

Happiness isn't!

That you can buy the rest, no longer matters when you can't buy this Trinity of life.

Senses

Come listen to the sound of the forest,

to fill yourself with love!

Come listen to the whisper of the stream,

to be filled with freshness!

Come smell the grass,

to inhale its scent!

Come relax in the shade of a walnut tree,

to feel its wisdom!

Come see the children,

to understand that happiness is in small things!

Come run through the flowers of the field, with grass up to your

knees,

to understand how light your body could be!

Come and read a book to better understand yourself!

Come play the whistle and let your ears tickle!

Come taste the honey of the hive,

to feel its sweetness!

Come to love,

for in Love is all this.

Do you love me?

Are you sure you love me?

How am I supposed to feel that way when you just tell me you want
to kiss me and to spend the night with me?

I'm asking you, then: will you drive me to the airport tomorrow
morning, it's two hours away? You know, I have to go.

You answer me: No, I can't!

Your carnal urges are trying to occupy a clear, healthy, and
dignified mind.

Your little soul, hidden by an immense shame, backs away.

For your carnal pleasures, sir, find your resources.

I am above every base need at nightfall.

You are pathetic and foolish!

But be proud of yourself for trying!

Two small and delicate hands

are the image of OUR unfailing love.

Perfect.

Beyond us.

They point to nowhere, in blurry, uncertain movements.

But in their sleep they're delicate. They sit together and tell a story

under a child's rosy cheek.

They rest because the search is too intense and the find too much.

We love you, beautiful child!

You are your father's supreme gesture of generosity

and your mother's supreme gesture of love!

Writing about love can be easy.

Living love can be hard.

An unrequited love burns hearts.

It wrings tears.

It moves words.

An unrequited love consumes energy

and doesn't let the moments add up.

An unrequited love holds you back.

It holds you back to hurt, to cry, to say meaningless words.

When, in fact, unrequited love is a lesson to remember.

It's you with your love and that's what you need to be most sure of.

If it happens that another Self and another Love resonate with you,

then it is Fulfillment.

If not, let your Love love you, and don't let your Unlove hurt you!

In a block of flats, a silhouette climbs with difficulty, leaning against
the crumbling wall.
She seems to mutter something, but I can't understand her.
I walk past her and continue up the cold grey stairs.
I don't want to disturb her moment with herself.
I can see her sadness gathered in the rain of tears
that stream down her face.
I dare to be silent.
A suffering cannot be interrupted.
I find out later that the man who had been her husband had
unceremoniously given her his Unlove, while Love had wrapped it
up nicely and given it to another.
For him it was happiness, for her, suffering.
Now.
Later, another becoming, with other loves and meanings...
We aren't seeking to identify the culpable; instead, we aim to
comprehend.
Everyone lives their life as their heart leads them...

The sunglasses conceal a cold, dark, perhaps even sinister look!

It's a gaze that refuses to communicate, ready to rebuff any attempts

at conversation with a scornful tone.

It's the cold look of unhappiness.

Why her and not another?

This cruel, repulsive gaze doesn't resonate with love.

Beneath it lies an abyss, one that seems to draw you in from the very

moment of your acquaintance.

Is there no one to teach her that kindness, a pure heart, and gentle

eyes attract positive things?

Is there no one to guide her, to rescue her from the abyss?

Is her love of so little significance?

Dear Woman, please realize that the love within you is seeking a

home

Help your Love find its cradle!

Throw away your sunglasses allowing the warmth of the sun to

enter your soul and fill you, for where there is warmth, there is life.

In the cold, everything remains frigid and sad.

I roll in a wave of happiness

... that my love gives me.

It knows about me that I love to be happy,

to laugh and wonder.

It knows that I love Love and that I often mistake myself for it.

"I take you in my arms, world, and tell you that I love you!"

For people like me, the world should be a big sun, bathing the fields

of flowers,

so that, in its fragrance, the purest form of Love may bloom.

The white of my love is clean;

It's a fragile dove that looks down on me.

My love has never descended the bridge of humility.

It has never carried weights,

It's not hunched.

My love needs no restorations, nor is it paved with stone.

My love is a free dove,

with blue eyes and diaphanous wings.

It doesn't care about air, fire, or water.

My white angel, my Love, comes from somewhere long ago and

descends only to bless me.

Every second of my life is a blessing.

Why is the lovely chestnut sheltered by a thorny and seemingly
unfriendly little house?
I adore its divine unveiling.
Even though its coat is adorned with spikes, the revelation is
captivating.
Its multiple colors, its sparkle, its halo—
A halo resembling a large, closed eye.
Within the eye lies the love of its phallic father and its radiant,
elegant mother.
The chestnut is the cherished child of an imposing, grand, powerful
father and a splendid, regal, captivating mother.
From the tree and its flower, the chestnut inherits mystery but not
their looks.
So, refrain from judging my love solely by appearances.
Behind an illusory appearance, my beauty is wrapped in mystery,
hailing from afar.

Give me time to go and find myself.

I don't have the money to pay you for my time.

I want to take the time to write my life's story on my soul.

I want to keep it as a memory for generations to come.

I want to leave my child with the legacy of my beautiful love.

I want them to read it and learn from it.

I want my child to know how to love beautifully, sincerely, and

honestly.

That's how love works, and my child embodies it.

I stand on the edge of a precipice, shouting the world's hatred.

I want it to swallow it up, take it deep into the earth, and consume

it.

I howl at the ugly Unlove that dehumanizes us.

I roar my despair.

Evil is too self-absorbed and has too many followers.

Where does love hide in these moments of dehumanization?

In the moments of these creatures possessed by evil, hate, and

ugliness?

The scorn of the universe has gathered to rage.

May the fires of hell consume Unlove,

and in its wake, may Love sprout.

I contest all the Unlove I non-accidentally sent you!

I contest all the Unlove that my Love has known!

I contest all the Unlove my heart has captured in its redness!

I contest all the Unlove that left me longing!

I contest all the Unlove that makes me melancholy!

I contest all the Unlove that brings me memories that embrace me
and never leave me!

I contest all the Unlove that left me a void that trembles in my eyes!

I contest all the Unlove with longing for old loves!

I contest all the Unlove that after years and years tries to return to
me!

I contest the Unlove that steals my nostalgia...

L - et your Love find its way!

O - vercome all Unloves alongside Love!

V - ibrate with your Love every time Love finds its shade!

E - njoy Love!